DECIPHER THE SMOKE

The content associated with this book is the sole work and responsibility of the author. Gatekeeper Press had no involvement in the generation of this content.

Decipher the Smoke

Published by Gatekeeper Press
7853 Gunn Hwy., Suite 209
Tampa, FL 33626
www.GatekeeperPress.com

Library of Congress Control Number: 2024948632

ISBN (hardcover): 9781662954597
ISBN (paperback): 9781662954580
eISBN: 9781662954603

DECIPHER THE SMOKE

Poems

NORA GUPTA

gatekeeper press™
Tampa, Florida

Praise for
Decipher the Smoke

Nora Gupta's chapbook, *Decipher the Smoke*, defies everything one would expect from a poet so young. Her poems are sophisticated, complex, nuanced, and original – each one a dazzling testament to her talent and dexterity with language. These poems witness and mourn, exhort and empower. There are poems written in elegy that manifest grief and loss as a tangible presence: "There isn't a word in English/ strong enough for what I carry now." There are also poems of identity and self-discovery. In a feat of syntactical magic, we follow a name as it travels from mouth to mouth in search of home "after/ it has walked out doors it cannot walk back in." The poet writes with defiant power and confidence, and despite the recurring themes of rage and loss (of which Gupta writes, "There's nothing sweet about that."), there are lullabies and songs, and sweetness abounds throughout - as illustrated in "caramel breath" and "holy molasses," "honeysuckle taffy" and "cinnamon eyes." These beautifully crafted poems will stay with you "…like a tooth/ from the church's mouth. Swallowed/ but never digested."

- Nancy Miller Gomez, author of **Inconsolable Objects**

Nora Gupta's Decipher the Smoke delivers us gorgeous, haunting odes to longing, youth, illness and grief, "an illness of its own", all while asking the question: what comes after? Gupta builds a world out of horizons, old and new, "blurring indigo and orange". A world that is at times ecstatic, at times ruinous, and always nourishing. These poems will dig themselves into the back of your skull and refuse to leave. I'm excited to see what she does next.

- Jordan Hamel, author of **Everyone is Everyone Except You**

Contents

I.

Suppose I Stopped Running

Butterscotch Manifesto

To the little girls with butterscotch black curls, fresh
     blonde waves, or even straight berry fizz, the girls
who will beam with the cellophaned elderflowers
     dropping their petals between sidewalk cracks, who wear
smiles flesh to stone, still shimmering, iridescent
     like the lips of market oyster shells—ignore
the pleas of men in pressed suits yelling
     from idling dentist office televisions.
You don't have to grow lusher in the charcoal
     black soil lining suburban gardens, you don't
have to smile every time a man waves. You can
     glare, ready to pierce Manhattan's sleepless frost.

You don't have to unwind your spine, don't have to
     laugh like spring wind, don't have to speak softly
as the fresh magnolia blossoms whispering across
     the crosswalks this time of year. You don't have to
be charmed by the hustling boys or the bustling boys, especially
     not the boys who will be boys. So, instead of letting
a cloud of cinnamon AXE corrode what beats

in your bosom, you can capture their pleas
     in a bottle—like laughter or the song of a spider web
after a boy kicks it into past tense. You can
     wear your moon-glazed eyes proudly, as each
ticklish tick of passing time echoes
     like the monsoon of possibilities within you.

Identity Blueprint with Cricket Music

Home is where your name belongs
     but not where it stays. As it was first
muttered under a mother's breath

         as she walked the freshly paved sidewalks—
           her palm on her stomach
     in her floral flowery dress—maybe

during the sticky August heat. And soon
         your name would travel
     into the preschool teacher's mouth

as she cautioned you—as you toddled over
       the cracked concrete, blossoming
         with the goo of black melting tar

and the yellow puffs of the nearly ripe
       dandelions. Then, once you've dug up
the browned bulb of childhood, your name will be

       bellowed out of your father's mouth
as he explains the logic of "4 x 4," your cheeks
         damp and tear-shiny because math

       never makes sense at that age. But home
is where your name belongs. Not
       in the winding beams of the family's

          circular oak table—chips and patches

of unfinished wood because you forgot
you can't clean wood with Clorox wipes. Not

on the walls where you proudly wrote
your name next to the line you drew
to mark your height an inch above

the previous mark—or the one before
or the one before that. Your name will find its home
after you are truly swallowed by the rays

of sadness and you understand what makes
a dead body worthwhile. Your name will find
its home after it has traveled in the watery spit

of spite and jealousy and you have listened to
the crickets at 2:00 a.m., whose music sounded
sweeter. A name will only find home after

it has walked out of doors it cannot walk back in.

Suppose I Stopped Running.

for Kate

Suppose I let your laughter twirl / my hair. Suppose my stomach didn't knot / as you laid bedridden blocks away, your heart readying / to stop. Suppose I stopped, let the soles of my feet bleed / into the road's endless tar, let the horizon blur / into the fields' grassy mouths. Suppose summer's silence sweetened / until it was too sweet to swallow, my caramel breath clouding / the air like cigar smoke. Suppose I filled / your maple-soft hand with mine. Suppose / your pulse didn't slow as mine / quickened. Suppose your eyelids, though touched / by gravity, never closed. Suppose I stopped running / and October never ended and orange-brown clung / to branches instead of tears yolking / my eyes. Suppose I sat in frosted grass and read / this poem into the ear of a tree stump. Suppose / I stared into the cooling coals of a forgotten fire pit until they were / your sea-black eyes. Suppose my words float off / this wrinkled page, suppose my rhymes glide / like silk. Suppose you really do hear me.

Elegy for Aunt Kate

a triptych

I.
The fear of Death was spoon-fed to me—
    the drear of black velvet drapes

over glossy wood coffins, heartbeats swallowed
    but never digested. Instead, I was

haunted by the wandering ghost of a question—
    What does it mean when your flesh turns

pale and your chest beats with only late autumn
    bare branches? They say Death is ugly,

for the frail—filled with hoarse cries, clammy
    clenched fists, holding a god who looks up

    with disdain. Still, she lived to
explore the bills of toucans and frost

the tips of mountains, and I bet her funeral will tickle
    the church floors as they creak with abandonment, as we steep

    in the liquor of mourning. I bet the pews will even soften
to splintering maple, poking through mauve

carpet—long faded, exposing patches of what's beneath.

II.
The last time I went to church, the harp strings trembled
        as the thurible swung like a brass pendulum. Sweet

smoke rose into the air with desperate prayer, icicles
        dripping across the evening's stained glass light. I watched

orange and blue and red sting my breath as the deep
        granite pillars reached through clouds to touch Heaven

with the holy molasses of song—yet as we sung, we descended
        into remorse, devotion. She was silent.

III.
At the funeral, Death was the only one
        who looked pretty in black, her laughter looping

through the hearth's crackling tinder. And after
        I confessed to the delirious sky, my amber fists—

        clammy and clenched, nails digging into
        God, soaked in the sweat of anguish—

I felt your heartbeat unfasten like a tooth
        from the church's mouth. Swallowed

        but never digested.

God's Bet

With every heaving breath Elpis took, I saw / God's bet
twinkling in her eyes. Her skin was / transparent—I could
see each quiver of her pulse, each hiss / of her garter-snake
veins—and I don't know / if this is the perennial of God's
will, but Mama told me / God's angels have swallowed Elpis,
leaving her / frostbitten. I still don't know / what god Mama
spoke of, but Papa says / Elpis is dying, he said her flesh
would tighten around her bones / as her eyes sank and her
legs crumbled. And I cried / until my eyes rang bloodshot,
the innocent glimmer / of Elpis between my matted lashes.
Elpis, matted / with tears and a scream prying open my lips. /
And slithering out my lips was the gutting sound of a mother
losing / her firstborn daughter, of my pupils shrinking / back
into my sockets and Elpis's hands wrinkling my breath / and
now when I put my palm in hers, my fingers interlace hers and
I see / the prairies she never visited, the daisies and dandelions
she braided / around her forearms, each petal falling with a
beat of her heart. And underneath her glazed eyes, pink roses
/ swirling with the black rot as summer parasites blossom,
blossom with the pain of a fresh bruise each time / I press it.

At Sunoco

Underneath the white LED lights, your veins slither
through your transparent skin. Your breath, labored
as it sifts gluttony into psychedelic honey, frosts

your face in sweat. Like a thick fog of smoke
settling around the Sunoco, we drift over
from a tangled, endless road. Roped with the aftertaste

of rush hour, our sweet Marlboros marry
the wind to the saffron, and the saffron to the summer-
burnt grass. The smell—even in memory, dusty

as the covers of fantasy novels we once decorated
with the music of cigarette butts, damp coupon cutouts.
Those were the days when I spent months catching your eyes

in discount dressing room mirrors, your hollow eyes
and fragile fingers tracing the moth-eaten frills
of everything I tried on for you on the Saturdays

you took me out after your chemo. I still see

flashes of blues and grays, even now, when I lie
in bed, picturing your sunken eyes drifting shut.
Ephemera. But now, my heart burns

through the guilt like the greasy salt of my 99¢ pizza,
like the buds of flame we dropped
into the grass—smothered by our feet, relit by the wind.

II.
First Witness

Poisoned Elegy (Green Apples)

I ate the fruits of loss and shame, not knowing
they marinated for weeks under the tree bark out back,

poisoned with words I was too young to understand. Bite
by bite, my life projected in front of me

from a silver beam, like Heaven had opened
its refrigerator door—and I wondered, *who is Loss, anyway*. Once

Aunt Kate passed on, and her body began
decomposing into the rich black molasses of memory, did she

really drip down my throat with sweetness

until my esophagus tingled as I slept? Bite by bite, my teeth
pierced bruises. Acid boogied on my tongue. Whenever

I leaned over the sink to wash out my mouth, I caught Loss
staring at me in the bathroom mirror, or at least a girl

who looked like Loss. She sat in the second stall—door
open, skipping second-period Health, waiting for me

to read the clock she cradled in her palms, which ticked
with each breath she took, until Shame walked in and claimed

the next stall. Shame, because I couldn't fully remember
a single memory with Kate—not the days we curled

into ourselves under thick wool blankets on the couch, as rain

drummed against the windows, not even days we filled
with awe as 婆婆 (pòpó) hummed to the sizzling symphony

of green peppers and pork over his oily pan. Shame watched me
walk right past Loss, embarrassed to hug Her when she showed up

on my first day of high school. I left Her arms hanging open—
Her eyes still hopeful, Her half-smile holding

the simple desire to watch old movies, to go shopping. Instead,
I stayed home, spent hours on calls with a boy

who never cared. And then, finally, I bit into the fruit

and Shame flamed across my chest until my skin bubbled
everywhere Loss had touched me, right there

over the kitchen sink—it flamed and bubbled until I agreed
to pierce the cold air of Fifth Avenue with our knife-tip

laughter, Loss and I, giggling at our reflections
rippling across the darkening store windows.

Elegy Through Snow

I track my body through snow
        brimming with the eternal glow
of grief—like tobacco, an unfinished stub
        melting its way to ash. Inside, succumbed
in hospice, your bony arms wrapped around my neck.
        Gold sparks rushed down my back, my body's way
                of knowing this would be the last time.

February's 6:00 p.m. sunset bites
        frozen poppies into my cheeks. I spray
rose hips & hibiscus in every room, but they wilt, even
        the dripping pastels claiming my fingertips. The dark
of night is an unfair fight—the sunset
        melting into its bowl of mint chip until only the frost-
tipped spoon remains. Without the sweet, I have
        only brown paper bags, compost feed to grieve.
I miss the monarchs we spent whole summer afternoons
        watching milkweed revel. They helped me escape
                what we knew.

In my bag, I still have
        your papaya-mango lip scrub. My palms rub honey-
lemon skin. You never got to hear of him,
        to see the glow of your bracelet beads
on my wrist, looping matte luminescence. My vows
        of devotion hang from my ears—saltwater
pearls, Purple Tahitians. They're imperfect, the foam
        of fate like seafoam clouding their centers, but they flake
the never-ending Chilean coastal landscape. And
                more importantly, they're ours.

Self-Portrait as Hello Kitty

Penthouse kitty, Hello Kitty. Gilded saxophone, crying to be used. Crying to exhale sweet notes, to make Billie Holiday dance. Notes slipping from loose bows, wrapping her last paycheck in sweat, in the marmalade that clung to the glass coffee table for months, in two shots of bitter, congealed punch. A punch of Mary Jane, sliding in between the pink satin cushions. One-hundred-dollar bills blowing dust across the peach-white couches, blowing into Uncle Sam's Sprite can. Bills scattered like puzzle pieces, like the 3rd St. Book Club scattered in pieces. Scattered like the feathers of goose down that escaped from just-fluffed pillows. Penthouse kitty, Hello Kitty. House parties, tapping feet, circling the beat. Circling the music on the speakers, flattening the ragdoll shag carpets into extinction. The cat's out of the bag now, the cigar's on Kitty's lips. Her eyes black and round—no longer cute, just drunk. The blue LEDs overhead drink the rage crackling in Kitty's claws. The rage that Kitty still scratches into the walls scratches through the pretty pink, the hot pink, the girly-girl pink universe. Penthouse kitty, Hello Kitty.

First Witness

Suppose I do change my life now. After.

Suppose I change my life with the flip
of the rusted penny kicked out from under
the diner's table—green paint fading, softened

oak. Imagine I bet our future on it, before
we learned what we know now. With every rotation
of that penny, now rusted to meaninglessness, a year

peeled from the shell of your life. At the end
of the day, who couldn't hate the illness shriveling
your innocent eyes, flattening your smile into shyness?

The grief bubbles along the underside
of my skin, an illness of its own—bubbles
burrowing under my pores. The first witness

is my mirror—I watch the scarlet letter brand
my blushing face, that *G*, grief's
Laffy Taffy—wishing I were just another

girl. Wishing for a beautiful smile, a hushed voice.
There are no greedy flames fanning inside
those girls, just sugary crushes and giggles crystallizing

their lips—melodies you would've loved
listening to, from the warmth of the living
room at Grandma's, tending to the soft shoots

springing from her tiny bamboo tree. And yet
one day, when grief visits, their eyes will
roll back and they will see. Every word

will fill their mouths with rotten fruit.
Would you know what to say?
What to do? There isn't a word in English

strong enough for what I carry now—

Dark Paradise

Under mounds of pillows
in a bed that wasn't mine, I swallowed
cotton-feathered clouds.

*

The stench of sweet cologne
lingers—artificial adoration probably
carrying the draft of a sinner

through the vent of my memories. Probably
because adoration always leaves
the door half-open.

*

I feel its gaze—in memory, I peer
from the corner of that cell
adoration held me inside for years, drunk

with narcissism, hidden pride. Captured
in a bottle—a dew-dipped spider web, freshly
broken—now, hiding in the shadows

of its own expectations. I hope
guilt runs oily down its fingertips, gathering
at its feet, filling with the unwelcome nectar

of thought. But you, you killed it
with a flick of the wrist.

*

The bitter embrace of longing I crave, a longing
softening into the wisp of a sincere kiss
left on the green sea glass—you will be

matte, the sweet scent of ashen cigars
crackling in this morning's dark
paradise, pulsing in pure imagination.

III.

OVERGROWTH

Overgrowth

Lush with weeds, it was a sorry excuse
for an oasis—shame
palpitating my chest, held by grass
cocooning the park in yellow, sprawling
through the alcove of rocks—each reaching to touch
the sky above the F-train, splintering
into headlights flecked with maple trees.

With the dandelions, I struggle
to escape rush hour's threat
to crack our concrete eggshell.
It's easy to understand, the challenge
of brown eyes and brown fingertips
slow roasting my lips. More than

Aesop's ripped fables, than the strobing
kiss of disco lights under last night's feet, I yearn
for liberation in the wake of temptation's
foaming tide, the music of lust electrifying
my pupils, dilated neon. The summer
stretching sea salt fingers across
my teeth. You said my mouth was
always too loud to chew, too dry to swallow.

We shed our overgrowth, the maple trees
dropping leaves where leaves should be. And you,
floating into the shade of my past, forgotten. I've forgotten
the bruises on my apricot knees, palms snaking
their own spine up my back. The stumble
in my blistering feet, the *bitch* in your laugh.

Even after the flowers release their adrenaline, the smog
still offers itself the autumn sky, still entangles
the sweetgrass with the streets. The city
is still the city, but now excitement grows—raw
& itchy—from the green of my chest.

Decipher the Smoke

As we watch the world descend
into the dimming torch of Lady Liberty
and the smog lining the desperate
faces of stars, we choose to defend the best
of the worst. I begin to wonder, to wander
into waters flowering with six-pack plastic
rings like delphiniums, petals loosed in wind—

on America's foam-licked shore, I'm still
doused in sunlight, watching the rainbow
slice kelp below the surface. But once
the men with white hair and eagle masks dyed
America two colors, the sea oozed until
decay hedged the silt of the shore we used to share.

When I inhale, pebbles of coal sizzle
with anxiety. When I exhale, the flame
spreads its scorching spores.

Now, it's a small glowing speckle.
Now, it's slowly losing light.

Osiris's scale trembles as hearts
harden to stone. Osiris leads us
to smoke we can't decipher—clouds
peeping the dusty sky, their still reflection
blanketing the shore, the sudden cotton foam.

It's November & They're Banning Books

Who she is
almost doesn't matter—only that she can't be
herself—not on the cover, not

in   front   of   this   class.   Dancing
on a milky toadstool, she's got to go—
she can't reveal her identity

until Chapter Four, questions bubbling
like Manila clams in low tide,
revealed. Her eyes

hide the velvet cinnamon
of November's cool kiss all autumn, moist
and littered, scattered across Chapter Seven

like a mural of dead leaves. In the real world
November's more of a cornucopia, filled
with snickering smoke, seasoned

with those cinnamon eyes as PTA moms burn
what they're afraid of—books
forbidden, sticky caramel chapters, sweetness

authentic, but charred. And ground and
glazed and torn—their disgust
with the Internet, their prideful teeth

sharp as needles, pressing through the skin of
what children shouldn't see, what children shouldn't
be, swallowing her smoking cinnamon eyes whole.

There's nothing sweet about that.

Candy Shop

I almost drowned at the beach yesterday
    after salt lapped at my shins and laid

cool kiss after cool kiss at my feet.
    I ran toward the horizon's blurring

indigo and orange. And once the rippling
    saltwater dried my palms, I watched

the horizon for greed's ungraspable nectar. But
    I didn't drift out to sea—seaweed stringed my ankles

like dead men's tales, keeping me
    tethered to shore. As wet sand sloshed

each step, the dull blade of dusk followed
    my body's tide with its shadow. And when

an innocent glow bled across the passion fruit
    stars, the August sunset pinned my head

to your shoulder. I almost drowned in your lullaby—
    that burning lullaby you poured into my ear

like sand, as the beach spun and twisted
    its honeysuckle taffy across Midas's kitchen.

And as that kitchen glittered with iridescent shells
    and watermelon flesh, I saw two pearls—symmetrical

beauty between blinks—two pearls that beckoned me
    to reach for the moon's bloodshot eye. Between

Aphrodite's gaze and the sun she painted for us, I knew
    in a matter of minutes, the giggling moon would wane.

Stem & All

after Jean-Baptiste Greuze's painting "The Broken Mirror"

Darling, hold your head high & step
over the shards of what's broken. Place

the nearest candle in your brass pricket, then open
your Indian rosewood dresser. The certificate of

your dowry has decomposed, the indigo
lettering now flakes of shivering ash. Dip your hands

into water; let the soot shimmer, let your husband's grease
float with the trembling ripples of your palms.

I am sorry his drool stained your satin to sin
before you could meet your first

love, before tenderness extended its hand. I know
you felt like a fool as the flower girl scattered

innocent petals & your sour mouth filled—I know
that was the moment you truly saw his face

for the first time. His cheeks, branded by
the false flush of the cross, cradled eyes flickering

with gluttony. But darling, hold your head up high
& greet him with deceit like a hydrangea

woven into your hair, stem & all.

Golden Hour

It was the hour of us, wrapped
in a siren's sun-slicked lullaby. The glow
whispering in your eyes, the faded mahogany
milled from the same maze
of autumn trees I spent my childhood
getting willingly lost inside, over
and over. The roasted chestnuts, the espresso
beans he ground into his stare
every morning. Caffeine sprouts the vines
stretching like fingertips across
the pinpricked sunburn he left me with—
sick, glowing. *Even the sun can't do that.* The sun
never left as much warmth on my cheeks
as the cinnamon tears I used to fill
the trenches of evening—they were
tangy, bittersweet as his leaves, draped
in velvet thorns, encasing buds of flame. As
your sparkling shadow leaning into mine, always
unchanged. As your rough bark, never
sun bleached. I believed the sun would never
bleach us, your hair forever coiling the marsh
of my pillow, perpetual sunburn painting
my journals, over and over—stinging
each sweet inhale. I believed the same
beige sweater he wore would never show
its wear, its neglect. The mangroves grew, guilty
as pleasure, the oranges shining before
dropping silently to the ground, before the Bowerbirds
picked them apart. It was like that—the juice, even
in golden hour, leaching into our maze of history.

Acknowledgments

Thank you to the editors of the following publications, where poems included in this chapbook appeared, often in earlier versions: *Girls Right the World, Glassworks, Notre Dame Review, Shō Poetry Journal, the Spotlong Review,* and *Zone 3.*

Thank you to the following organizations, who recognized poems included in this chapbook: the Bronx High School of Science, the City College of New York, Gannon University, Gigantic Sequins, the National Council of Teachers of English, the National Scholastic Art & Writing Awards, the National YoungArts Foundation, the New York Life Foundation, Princeton University, and Smith College.

Thank you to my creative writing mentors, whose careful craft instruction and life advice have sharpened my navigation of the literary world, and the world beyond it: Peter LaBerge, Jamie-Lee Josselyn, Simon Shieh, Lisa Hiton, and Nino McQuown.

Thank you to my brother, who never fails to find the best, uncanniest times to pester me into laughter.

And most of all, thank you to my parents, who have found their own ways to support me.

About the Author

Nora Gupta is a student poet at the Bronx High School of Science. Her poems have appeared in *Girls Right the World, Glassworks, Notre Dame Review, Shō Poetry Journal, The Spotlong Review, Zone 3,* and elsewhere. Her poetry and prose have received additional recognition by the National Scholastic Art & Writing Awards, the National YoungArts Foundation, Princeton University, Gannon University, and Smith College, among others. Nora is also the editor-in-chief of *Double Yolk,* a publication featuring poets of color that shines a light on their creative processes. She lives in Queens, New York.